To
Jamil'

MW01503407

I Did It for Her

Her

Daisy Plaza

Contents

Dedication

This book is dedicated to my daughter Mikeala King and Ericka Caban

A Note from the Author

These events are accurate to the best of my ability. My memories of these events might be different from what others remember. That's what trauma does.

This is not a book of bashing. It's a book of education. It does include other people but it's not about them. It's about how I healed from the experiences. And I'm sharing it to help others.

Introduction

Her final words were a promise I knew I had to keep. I have to tell the story...MY story.

Pieces of me were stripped away leaving me damaged and broken. Battle along with me as I struggle through a manipulative and abusive marriage while trying to maintain an unconditionally loving family. Watch how I transition my trauma and fear into pure love and strength.

I had to. It was the only way to be a supportive mother to my four children and show them how to be strong, even in the most unfortunate situations.

It's time to take back the life that I so rightfully deserve, and I'll show you how.

1

Ericka

"You have to tell your story."

My son Schamar brought Ericka over so we could all meet her. At first she didn't speak much, she kept to herself. She came off as very quiet and with an attitude. He brought her over for our New Year's party. She and my son looked so in love. She was 16 and he was 17. Both of them were in high school but didn't attend the same one. At first, I felt she was always upset and mad about things for no reason...Boy was I wrong.

The more we spent time together, the more she started to open up. We started having conversations about her life. My GOD was she broken! We celebrated every holiday together and our New Year's party was so much fun. All of my kids and grandkids loved her.

It took several years for her to open up to me but I'm so happy and grateful she finally did. She started to sleep over all the time. The older kids were like, "Why can she stay here? You never let a girl stay in the house! You never let none of us do that!" I would just laugh. Schamar was the baby. I was a lot more lenient. I felt that he was responsible and never gave me a hard time and always asked.

We then created a relationship. I looked at Ericka like she was my other child. She would come into my room late at night and we would talk for hours. My son would say, "Damn, can I have her back?" We would all start laughing.

These conversations became heartwarming. She opened up to me about so many things she encountered as a child. It started to sound so familiar. I would understand why she was the way she was: reserved, emotional, angry, and sometimes happy just depending on the day. We would both laugh and cry together.

She was so hurt and broken. I just wanted her to be happy and loved. She felt that she wasn't loved or protected enough. So I promised myself I would show her differently and make her feel that she was a part of our family. She would get in a dark place and wanted not to live. This happened often. She had started drinking at a very young age. We discussed that, too. She would do good for a while, then go back to drinking to numb herself from things she felt like she couldn't handle. There were many times when she stated that my son saved her. I found out later that Schamar worried about her a lot.

They went to each other's prom. We were all so happy and excited. They looked perfect and happy. I made sure they had everything they wanted. They graduated from high school. Schamar was a year ahead. When she graduated she decided she wanted to go to college and she got into UCONN. I wasn't surprised. She was so intelligent and wanted so much in life.

She wanted to be a teacher. I was so proud of her. She lived on campus her first year. Schamar would stay in her dorm as much as he could. He would never be home.

The summer after her first year at UCONN, Ericka and Schamar decided to get their own place. I was so proud of them. They moved in on September 1st. I was right there with them, the annoying mom helping and taking pictures. They bought all their own stuff and settled in quickly.

She would call me and ask me to sleep over on the weekends. I came whenever she asked. We watched Netflix, ordered pizza, and laughed. We would talk about relationships, her wanting to be a teacher, and books she loved to read. She would buy so many books. She loved to talk about horoscopes. During this year we were very close. She was doing great in school and loved her new place.

But she would get in a dark place once again. With school, working, and watching her siblings during the week, life became overwhelming. Her grades were dropping and she felt like something had to give. I told her it would get better. I would encourage her to go back to counseling and that everything was going to be okay. She had assured me that she was okay and she was going to figure it out.

We got into many discussions about me writing a book because I would share so many stories with her and she would say, "You have to tell your story."

She created my book outline and guided me with great pointers. We would talk about opening our own business. I loved designing and she loved doing makeup. She would do mine all the time and she made me feel beautiful. We wrote down all of our ideas. She would always question and doubt herself. I always told her she was amazing and was great at whatever she decided to do.

In May we decided to go to Florida. It was our first trip away together and we couldn't wait to go. Me, Ericka, Schamar and my son Justin went. We were excited and couldn't wait to get there. My God, did we have a great time! We got an Airbnb. It was huge and beautiful. We laughed, partied, ate, and went to the beaches. My favorite place we went to was Volcano Bay. We went on almost all of the rides but tube riding was our favorite. My son ended up losing his glasses in the water. All we could do was laugh. That week went by so fast.

When we got back home, they decided to take a break from each other. I didn't know why and I never asked. She decided to move in with her mom and Schamar came back with me.

I was sad but they had to figure out what was best for them. We still kept in contact of course.

Three months later that all changed.

I thank God every day for her last text to me. She wrote that she never wanted to disappoint me and that she was going to get help and do better.

I knew she struggled with depression and didn't want to live. My son tried to save her many, many times.

I thought that maybe I didn't do enough or maybe I could have said more than I did. The truth is she tried to save herself and in the end life just caught up with her.

Ericka expressed that we gave her a reason to live as we showed her unconditional love.

I'm writing this story because her last words were that she loved me as if I were her other MOM, and she said, "You have to finish your book."

I promised her I would.

She believed my story had to be told. So, here it is!

2

Innocence and Betrayal

The Annawan project was the place where it all started. It was just my mom, my brother and I. My brother and I shared a room. We were very close. He was only two years younger than me. We had bunk beds. I had the top bunk of course. We had every toy you can think of.

My mom was always fussing for us to clean our room. We had roaches and mice there but it was home. My mom was very meticulous about keeping it clean.

In our living room, we had two long pieces of plastic and bricks that held the record player, speakers, and some plants. Music was very essential growing up. On Saturday mornings we were woken up by loud music and Mom telling us to get up and clean.

I remember seeing my mom always upset, aggravated, stressed, and yelling. She was always anxious and always worried about everyone.

My mom didn't drive and we had no car, so we took the bus everywhere. I found that to be more adventurous. She always found a way for us to take trips to parks, boat rides, and lake houses in the summer.

We took the bus in the mornings to school, then my grandparents picked us up from daycare every day. We couldn't wait to get home because we wanted to be with our friends. My mom's friend Titi Miga lived in the building across from us. She would babysit us sometimes until my mom got home from work. We loved it there. Her family treated us like we were a part of their family. To this day we are still family. We created the best friendship.

My brother and I would ride our bikes everywhere with our friends. Mine had a yellow seat with daisies on it! We would sneak out of the complex and ride over to the cookie factory that was about 15 minutes away. We would be able to steal packages of cookies and eat them before going back home so we wouldn't get caught. My brother and all our friends would have to get home before our parents got home from work. So many times, we would be rushing back and would fall off our bikes. We had so many scrapes and bruises, but we would just all laugh and do it over and over again. I will say many times we would get caught but that ass whoopin' would be worth it.

The complex was not very big; there were four brick buildings and the parking lot was small. I would love to come home from school to see what we were going to do. We were always outside and we would have different choices of what we were going to do. Like playing Road Runner. *Beep beep!* We would yell, "Road runner!" and the others trying to hide would yell,

"Beep beep!" for hours. It would echo out and all you could hear was laughter. We would play hide and go seek. It was hilarious cause we would hide in the buildings and they would never find us and we would have to eventually just give in and come out.

Opening the water hydrant was the best part of the summer. It would be so hot. As soon as that cold water hit our skin, all we would do was run and scream and push each other in the water for hours. We never wanted the day to end. The only rule we had was to be in the house as soon as the street lights came on.

When I attended elementary school, my brother and I were lucky enough to go to daycare right across the street. It was always fun. They provided snacks and lunches in the summer times. My favorite was lemon pudding. It's the best I ever had. They celebrated holidays there for all the kids. The best one was Christmas. They had gifts and food and Santa and music and even presents for us. Every time my grandparents would pick us up, my grandfather would have a surprise for us—bubblegum and all sorts of candy. We got to hang out with them and that was the best part.

School was great. Our school was not in one building. They looked like little houses made out of brick; they were called MIAs 1-6. We had to walk to each one for our classes. I was at the top of all my classes. I won all kinds of awards from history to science to best vocal. (Funny. Now I can't sing to save my life!) I won the best poet contest in the state. I got straight A's. I loved playing double Dutch with my friends. I was on top of the world.

Life was so simple. Life at home got more chaotic as my brother and I got older.

Our father wasn't really in our lives at all. He divorced my mother when I was a toddler and went on with his life. He married another woman and had two daughters. That didn't last too long either.

We would see him here and there. He was never there to help support or even provide for or protect us. He was never at any school events, any of our birthdays, or even holidays. And the little bit of times he picked us up he would bring us to our grandmother's house, so did that really count?

The only memory he left us with was his corny jokes that we loved and his laughter. The other side of him was being on drugs like coke and heroin, and us reading an article in the *Hartford Courant* of him stealing and being behind bars. The fun times he did give us were when he was doing well we would go fishing.

My Abuela Maria enabled my father by doing everything for him. He never had to take accountability for anything because my grandmother cleaned up his messes. For our birthdays and Christmas she would buy us everything to make sure we were happy and stated it was from her and my dad. I saw her many times in pain, always making it easy for everyone else but herself. She drank a lot of alcohol to numb herself. I believe it helped her cope with everything. Our happy moments together were in the kitchen. She cooked whatever we wanted. She loved us unconditionally. I felt she always tried to make up for what my father didn't do for us.

My brother on the other hand looked at him as a perfect father because whatever time he got was good enough for him. My brother wanted to live with him so bad.

My brother was the funniest person ever and he was always in trouble. My mother couldn't handle him at all. I found myself protecting him from bullies in school and from my mother at home. She yelled all the time. Hitting us was her answer for everything because that was all she knew.

I was raised with tough love. She yelled and kicked our asses with belts and no clothes on. This was the norm in my home. My brother was a difficult child but he got it the worst.

My mom had one boyfriend who I hated the most as he thought it was ok to pinch my brother and I in the back seat of the car if we didn't listen. My mom was in the car and never said anything, just participated. I feel I should have been protected more. On one occasion he beat me with a belt when I didn't eat all of my food. I didn't understand why no one stopped him. Why didn't anyone intervene? No one said shit to my mom either. One of the men she dated was a good role model, one I considered my father figure. He was there for me even when I became an adult and he guided me with several things in my life.

It was during this time that I also had my innocence stolen from me. By someone right next door.

One of our neighbors was a woman with three children. My brother and I got along with them and we all became friends. One of the older children happened to like women. That was not normal for us to see or hear but we never judged. Until she started to touch me and try to kiss me. I was afraid and I couldn't tell anyone. She looked at me with a disgusting look that scared me. She would touch me inappropriately. This happened for a long time. Even after my mom sent me away to a private school she tried to violate me but she couldn't. I was protected being in the home, no one could just walk in.

In that moment she stole my innocence, trust, and the way I looked at people. I became a different person with fear and anger. I could never trust anyone again.

My mom knew she liked women but not what type of person she was. She never knew what she was doing to me. I was afraid to ever say anything.

3

Unprotected

So many things happened between the ages of 13 to 17, that I have trouble remembering what order things occurred in. I think my brain might be trying to protect me from remembering.

When I was around 13 years old we moved to Whitmore Street on the first floor of a house. My aunt and cousins lived on the 2nd floor.

I thought life was going to be better, but nothing really changed. I thought with this new year and new school it would be filled with new beginnings and new friends. My brother and I did meet all new friends there that would eventually become family.

I was attending junior high. I remember being teased all the time because I was very skinny and had psoriasis. They would call me "Rashidy Ashidy." They would yell, "Don't touch her! You will catch her cooties!" I would cry all the time, but after a while, I just didn't care anymore. I just stayed to myself.

I felt like I'd lost everyone.

I did have my cousins, though. My cousins and I were always together. There were nine of us on my mother's side and three on my father's side. We were always super close through death, laughter, and lots of ups and downs. We stuck together no matter what.

We would see each other every weekend and every holiday at my grandparent's home. We looked forward to talking about everything. As we became older we were even closer. Our childhood was full of love from our grandparents, but also abuse we all endured behind closed doors from our parents.

My cousins were always with me. We protected each other no matter what. We had fun together. We got into shit together. We always felt we were all we had. I felt like I had to protect them. I tried to not let anything happen to them. I was the 2nd oldest and I felt that I had to do that to the best of my abilities.

Our parents were all very strict. What we had in common was we all had parents who were verbally and sometimes physically abusive. I saw and heard so much, it made me sad and angry. I would say it was the norm but we were young and really couldn't say or do anything.

I didn't like being home most of the time. I loved being with my grandparents and my aunt Zeny. She spoiled us. Zeny protected me a lot and would defend me even when I misbehaved. She was our favorite.

My Abuela Isabel was so important to me. She was inspiring, loving, structured, disciplined, and fought for what she believed in. She protected us at all costs. She endured a lot as a child and in her upbringing. She believed in family being together and being there for each other no matter what.

I was lucky to be able to have lived with her on multiple occasions. When I was around 14, she even took me to her home which she still owned in Puerto Rico. I remember it had a small living room, a tiny kitchen, and two bedrooms. There was no bathroom. The shower was outside in the back. There were three cement walls and a metal door to cover the front of it for privacy. The toilet was out front in the outhouse which I hated. I found it spooky but that was the bathroom. I remember a large barn in the back I would sneak off to and play in. What was crazy is that my grandparents and their five children lived in it until they built their home.

I got to meet more of her family including her brothers and her nieces and nephews. What a great time. They could hardly speak English and I struggled with Spanish but we made it work.

She never spoke about her life and the pain she went through and not being raised with her brothers and sister, not even about her mother dying when she was only a child. I looked up to her and she inspired me to be who I am today: a mother, a woman with a purpose. She showed me no matter how hard it got to not give up. She was selfless and always put everyone before herself but don't get it twisted she was not the one you wanted to mess with. She took no shit.

4

This Is Not My Home

I was an Honor student who won every award and never got in trouble in school until I went into the 7th grade. Then shit just changed. New school, new friends, new environment. I lost a little of myself.

Seventh grade did not go well. For 8th grade, my mom decided to put me in a private Christian school in Springfield, Massachusetts. I guess my mom thought this was a good idea. I don't recall my mom explaining why I had to go there. I never understood why. I don't ever remember my mother explaining to me why she made that decision.

It was so scary to walk into a new place I had never been to before. The stairs were all wood with very wide dark and tall ceilings.

I was introduced to four girls. Everyone said, "Hi." They were in one huge room where they stayed in on the right-hand side that had a fireplace and their own beds.

I had my own room up the hall. It was very small with a bunk bed and one dresser. I got to stay in my room alone.

I hated it there. It felt like a huge mansion. I felt scared and alone and had no one to talk to. I thought to myself, *how can any mom do this and sleep at night?*

There was a white couple who played the mom and dad roles. They were strict with no communication really. If I didn't do what they said, I would have to stay in my room.

They had rules on what time we ate and what time we went to bed. I guess that was their way of having structure. I don't ever recall being able to call any of my family and speak to them and none of them called me.

I was taught when shit got hard I had to figure it out. I was a loner.

I only remember a girl named Dawn that I considered my friend. We would go outside but most of the time I would just sit there alone.

I was told whatever happened in the home stayed in the home.

We would have transportation from the home to our school, which was a Christian school. We had to wear uniforms, with a white shirt and a pleated skirt. It was also very dark, all wood everywhere, like the house. Long hallways with wood floors. The stairs would creak loudly as we walked to each class.

One of the classes had a long wooden table with about 14 chairs where we would rehearse bible verses. It was not like a normal class with desks and chairs.

My favorite time in one of the classes was down the hall where I learned to play chess. My teacher was cool and the only one I remember. Their food wasn't good because I can't even recall what we ate for lunch.

After I had been there for a couple of weeks, the neighbor who had touched me had somehow found out where I was. I was outside sitting on the grass. I noticed someone standing outside of the property. I realized it was her!

She kept showing up. She would watch me from the street. I lied to the staff and told them I did not know her. She scared me, but I knew she could not get to me.

I felt alone and pissed off. I recall never talking to my mom except on weekends. I started to misbehave. They started not letting me go home on the weekends. If they stated I misbehaved my mom took their word and never asked me what happened!

Then I was really alone. Not even allowed to go home on the weekends to see my family. I was so angry at my mother for this. She never listened.

That was the longest year of my life. Thank God I was going into high school.

5

Left Behind

I was 16 in high school, not doing well, misbehaving, living with my mom and my brother.

One day, we were home hanging out with friends like always. It was a day in September. The weather was cool but nice to be outside. But it turns out it would be a day I would never forget.

"Get in the house right now!" my mother screamed. "Something happened to your father, you need to go call your grandmother."

As I walked into my house, I was confused, but curiosity kept me moving toward my mom's bedroom where the phone was. As I dialed my grandmother's number, my heart started to race...faster...and faster.

"Hello." My cousin answered the phone.

"Where's my dad?!" I shouted.

A few seconds of silence turned into a lifetime.

My cousin finally said, "Your father's dead."

*Thump! T*he phone fell right out of my hands as I screamed, "NOOOO!"

My vision became blurred as hundreds of tears streamed down my face. My knees dropped to the ground and the world around me began to crumble right before my eyes.

My brother fell to the floor crying not understanding why and how this could happen. My father had been killed in a car accident, and I never got to see him because his casket remained closed.

I remember looking down at the closed casket and the pain was unbearable. I still had so many questions. WHY HIM? Was he really in the casket? Maybe they made a mistake.

I felt like I never got closure, but one thing that I will always remember is the last conversation my father and I had over the phone. Our last words to each other were "I love you."

Two days prior my father had called to speak to us. My brother was so happy because my dad said he was going to take us fishing. My dad also told my brother that they were planning on having him live with him. My dad told me that he loved me and I told him that I loved him. I would have never imagined that would be the last time I spoke to him.

I was taught life goes on. We were taught to never talk about it or get proper counseling. I felt that none of my family from my mom and my dad's side were ever there for me or my brother. My dad wasn't there as much as he should have been for me and my brother but the times we did have I was grateful for. With all the things that happened to me after he died all I could think about was, *if he was still here would he have protected me? Would my life have been different?*

As the events unraveled we found out my father had a day off from work and decided to go to Avon with his friend. The story was they stole some things that were later found in the trunk of his car. He was on his way back home and on Avon Mountain where he decided to pass a car in front of him. He never saw the car coming in the opposite direction. He hit the woman head-on. The woman was injured but OK and my father's car was totaled. His friend went through the front windshield and died instantly. My father crushed his chest on the steering wheel. My father was transported to the hospital where they stated he would have been a vegetable if he survived.

I was so angry that the woman that he hit survived and walked away with just a dent in her car and simple neck injuries, but he died! I felt that was so unfair. She was old, I thought, why couldn't she be the one that died? My father was only 36, what about us and our family?! I didn't understand why this had happened to him. A couple of days later, the *Hartford Courant* showed the picture of his car. It was devastating. I was in complete shock to see my father's red car split in half. I held onto the newspaper because that was all I had left of him.

After that, my life just got worse. The day of the funeral there were so many people there. So many people were crying. My grandmother never showed up. I remember being in the car following the hearse and just crying. I promised myself to never go back to the cemetery.

We went to visit my grandmother after everything and she just sat by the window waiting for my father to come home. She was in denial and was never the same again. She would see a red car parked or driving by and she would say, "Your dad is here. He is coming up soon. You guys will see." She never spoke about the accident and we never brought it up. Many years went by and she became fragile and old quickly. She was never the same.

Her face was soft and full of wrinkles and her hair went all gray. I didn't visit much because things were so different.

I didn't give a fuck about anything or anyone. All my choices were careless and my life spiraled out. I started running away. I did not want to be home. I would stay at a friend's house, not caring how much that hurt my mom.

Although I didn't want to believe that he was gone, the reality was that this did happen and now I had to figure out how to live without ever being able to see him again.

6

No One Hears Me

Summer had started and we were always hanging out doing shit we weren't supposed to. There was a guy I knew and he liked me. I thought I was able to trust him. He had asked me to go with him. He said he needed to show me something behind a school. Mind you, I used to break into this school with friends to go swimming, so I didn't think nothing of it and I went with him. We got to the back of the school and his friend stayed in the front of the school. I wasn't sure why, and I didn't bother to ask. He then started to forcefully kiss me and he touched me in places. I told him to stop but he didn't.

As I yelled I held tight to my shorts so he couldn't unbutton them. I screamed but no one could hear me. I begged him. I told him I was still a virgin and I didn't want to lose my virginity this way. He said he was going to get what he wanted but I fought him. I punched him, slapped him, yelled. He was strong but I was not letting him get the best of me. I couldn't even tell you how long I was back there for but it felt like it was never going to end. I knew my friends would sooner or later come looking for me. Or at least I hoped they would.

Then I heard someone asking his friend where I was. He was loud so I started screaming louder.

One of my friends came running in the back. "What the fuck is going on?" my friend said.

I cried and yelled, "He is trying to rape me!"

Of course, he denied it and ran. His friend was in the front the whole time as the damn lookout. He knew what his friend wanted to do to me! I ran and as my tears ran down my cheeks, I told them, "Get them both and fuck them up." We chased them but they got away.

The crazy part, the one that saved me, ended up being the love of my life and the father of my first two children.

7

Broken

My life went into a spiral that I had no control of. I really didn't care about any consequences. I was fighting all the time and failing my classes. I wasn't listening to anyone so I had to repeat the 9th grade. I thought it was going to be better but then halfway through the year, I was just getting worse. They decided to expel me and sent me to a school for students with behavioral problems. This school was supposed to be structured for students who they decided could not be in a regular school. And they were supposed to help us with dealing with our anger and being able to work in our classes. But that was not the case. We would walk in our class with food and beverages. Teachers had no control over us. I did whatever I fucking wanted. We never learned shit in any of these classes.

At this time we had people from Park Street in the South End of Hartford and kids from the Avenue in the North End of Hartford. You kinda had to choose what side you were going to be on. The crazy part was that the Hispanics would say that I wasn't Spanish enough and the Blacks embraced me. Culturally I always felt I was a part of both the Hispanic and the Black culture.

We would be in class and it wouldn't take long before someone started some shit. Like someone would come in and snatch a bag of chips out of someone's hands and *BOOM* there goes a fight. Someone grabbed a kid by his throat and put his head through the damn window. This was normal to see and do.

When walking through the hallway to get to our next class, someone would make a comment and then "Here we go again!" It was another fight.

The teacher couldn't even stop it. We would just laugh. There were no consequences. We got away with fighting, smoking weed, and disrespecting the staff. This type of school was awful. It never helped us, it made us worse. It seemed like the structure was not executed or even designed to help us. I never learned anything in that school but I made a lot of friends. Of course I passed without even doing the work. I didn't put in any effort as I felt that they didn't require it.

I became another person filled with anger. I was lost. I fought in school suspension to expulsion. I met the father of my first two children. He was my first love. I have to say I was only 16 and had no clue what love was. He was perfect. He was 6' 3", kind and was there for me when my father passed. He took me to his prom. He was on the football team and he said all the right things. He protected me. He had saved me from a man that tried to rape me. He was my first as I lost my virginity at the age of 17 by him. He made me feel safe. Then everything changed over time. He was not who I thought he was.

When I was 17, I found out I was pregnant with my first child. I had to start a new school the following year. I was sent to a school for young pregnant girls. I didn't last long there either as I fought all the time. I then quit school. I was living at home with my mom and stayed with her when I had my son. Eventually, I moved in with my son's father and his parents until my son was 10 months old and I was pregnant again. We then decided to get our own place and everything changed.

He became very abusive and told me that I would never be shit. "Stupid bitch nobody loves you, not even your mother. You are lucky I am even here." We were together for about three years and lived together for about a year. He cheated and he lied. We had two children together that he had no intentions of taking care of.

We argued a lot. He started to be home less and less. He then had an attitude that he didn't care and he was living his own life. During an argument he took my child out of the crib and threatened to throw him down the stairs while the other one watched me scream, begging him not to hurt my son. He finally gave him back to me and walked out of the house.

One day he came home and said that he was in love with another woman that was in college. He said she had more to offer and he was leaving us. What could I do? I became angry. I wanted to kill him with his own gun. I ran upstairs to get it and then ran out to shoot him. I wanted to hurt him like he had just hurt me. He got in the car and drove off.

What was I going to do with two kids alone? I was 19 with two kids, no job and I hadn't even finished high school.

I never saw the signs or even knew what to look for in a relationship. I thought this was what people did when they were with someone. I never knew the difference. I thought there should be disagreements and frustration as this was normal. I was tired and I had no one to turn to.

One day we were arguing. I told him I was going to call the cops. He became so angry he grabbed the telephone from the wall and hit me in the head. I raised my hands to protect myself. He did it over and over so I wouldn't call 911. My children were in their bedroom. They were not old enough to know what was going on. My screams alerted the neighbors. They called the police to help me. He then locked himself in the bathroom stating he was going to hang himself! Fuck! I felt so lost.

I blamed myself. I thought it was my fault I did not do enough for him. Maybe I didn't love him right. Shit, I didn't know how!

The police showed up and so did his parents. The cops let him leave because his brother was a cop so nothing was done. No consequences. No one gave a fuck about me or my children. His parents took him with them and left me there fucked up with my two kids.

I found myself living alone there with my kids for a short time. I went on welfare because their father never came back to help us. My cousins and my brother started to come hang out more and I started partying, drinking, and smoking. Of course, they all thought I was the cool one. What I was was a fucking mess! I was the oldest and I allowed them to do whatever they wanted in my home. I had no boundaries.

Not too long after I was evicted and this is where everything just got worse. I borrowed my friend's car to go to the store and had her stay with my sons. I had no license and I had weed on me to sell and of course I got pulled over. I was arrested for lying and having no license. I had weed in my panties so they never found it. I stayed locked up overnight. I didn't get to call anyone til the morning. No one knew where I was. I got released in the morning with a promise to appear. I had to hurry as it was also my moving day. I arrived home and the damn moving truck was already there. I wasn't prepared and I was tired. Well, we threw everything in the U-Haul and I moved into another place in Hartford where I made all of the wrong decisions for me and my children.

8

Open Arms

I wanted and needed support that I never received from my family. I didn't know what I was going to do next with two kids. So I made friends with the wrong crowd doing shit I knew was not good. But they showed me love and they weren't even family.

This is when I got involved with a gang. I saw more deaths and beatdowns than I could ever imagine.

1993 was the craziest year of my life. My boy's father had left me. I had been evicted from our home. I ended up renting an apartment in Hartford off of Park Street.

My brother introduced me to one of his female friends. We had met at a party we went to. She introduced me to hundreds of gang members. I thought to myself, this is crazy. By the end of the night, they had asked me to join them.

I said no at first but within a couple of weeks, I joined the gang. They had girls beat me down to initiate me. It felt like an eternity. I was told if I could handle it I would be in. So I did and just like that I had a new family.

People asked me why I would do this if I had a good family.

My answer was, "OK, so where are they? I have nothing and no help." I felt alone. The gang felt like family and there was no judgment.

You see, at first I thought it was cool to be a part of something even though it wasn't right in anyone's eyes. I smoked weed and drank 40 ounce beers in the morning and partied every night. The streets became more important. Everyone came over. I was so popular but it was in the most negative way.

At 20, with two kids, damn I thought *this was life,* but really I was becoming more damaged.

I had no clue what was really going to happen.

Coming home to no lights and no heat or hot water was painful. Who could I turn to without feeling judged or being told to get my shit together? That was what I was trying to do! I had to figure out how to make sure my kids were ok. Fuck me! I decided to steal electricity from the hallways to light up my living room and play the TV for my children. I had to swallow my pride and I begged my neighbor to let me and my children bathe there.

I started selling weed to feed my children. I was on welfare and the money was not enough. I couldn't get a job because no one would watch my children. If anyone ever said it was easy or I didn't need help, believe me, that shit is a lie. Their father never cared and never helped.

Having nothing to eat, the money I made from selling drugs got me enough to buy food to feed my two kids and I barely ate. As long as my children had no idea what we were going through I felt like that was all that mattered. I made it as normal as possible for them.

I thought nothing would ever happen to me or my kids.

My life started to spin out of control. I fell in love with a gang that could never reciprocate what I was giving. We were there for their benefit and they wanted control over territories we didn't even own.

9

Making the Wrong Decisions

I went ass-backwards in my life at this time. In my apartment, under my bed, I had over 25 machine guns, TEC-9, 9 Glock handguns, 22s, and many more. This was not OK but I did what I thought I needed to at the time.

I fell in love with one of the members, and I felt he protected me and loved me. I thought nothing would ever happen to me or my kids as long as he was around. We were put on missions to find a certain person or people and jump them. We would rent a U-Haul truck and jump in the back and pull up where we were told to fight.

I was involved in many meetings in Pope Park where we spoke about who we would be terminating and adding as new members and what other missions we needed to do. I watched many of them get beatings to join. I saw the ones we terminated get beat down, even with crushes until they seized and were hospitalized.

We went to a party at a project where we knew certain individuals would be. Our job was to jump these people and make sure we won. To tell you the truth, we were never told why. We just had to get it done. I was told while walking in the streets, "Go hit her and beat her ass." I did it with no questions asked.

So many were hurt and killed during this time. It became the norm.

I knew I wanted more in life and this was not it.

10

So Much Blood

One night all the gang members got together. It started off as a party. We were celebrating a newfound peace in the community. I was told to meet at a hall for a meeting with another local gang to discuss how we would stay peaceful and not go against each other. So we all met up at a club on Park Street.

There was one way in and one way out. It was so packed that night. The music was loud and everyone was talking and having a great time.

Then it happened.

I was standing by someone who pulled out a gun. He pointed it up in the air and *boom,* a gun shot up in the air. It was so loud. Then there was nothing but silence and confusion.

It had been a setup! The pool balls and cue sticks were thrown and chairs were used to hit people over their heads and hit their faces. Stabbings even happened. In my mind I didn't want to die but how was I going to get out? Men were beating on men and even on women. I fought like I had never fought before.

I kept slipping and didn't know why.

I looked down. There was nothing but puddles of blood.

So much blood. In my mind I was thinking today might be the day I was going to die.

You couldn't even see the floor that was once white.

I ended up in the bathroom still fighting, hitting girls' heads on the sink. There was a woman who was being beaten and stabbed in her back from the top of it to the bottom. Everyone was running, fighting until we all finally pushed through the doors. There was more screaming and more gunshots being fired in all directions.

We finally got out of the building and ran to the car. We grabbed our weapons and drove home where we thought it would be safe as all hell broke loose.

This was just the beginning of a full-blown war. That is the day the war began in the summer of 1993 between both gangs.

While at home all we could hear was gunshots. I had to lay down in the dark with my two children hoping no one would come into my home.

Some of the gang members at the time showed up with cars and protection to get me and my kids out. My friend said, "You can't stay here. Get your kids."

If I stayed home there would be a chance that the gang members would rush into my home and murder me and my children.

I was then escorted to a hotel where we stayed for about three days. We were kept safe there.

This war was so bad and just kept going. Many people were dying. There were so many funerals and innocent people were paying for this decision that was made. Just going outside I had to watch my back. I had the mentality of *I will get you before you get me.* I rarely visited my own family because I didn't want them involved in my shit. I didn't want them to get hurt because of my choices. Going to the store, the gas station, anywhere, we could be shot at and even jumped.

Another incident I'll never forget was on the corner of Broad Street. We were all in the apartment building in one of the rooms when I heard a gunshot. It echoed through the room. I yelled, "What the hell?" I ran to the window and looked outside. Everything was in slow motion. I saw a man that I thought was so nice to everyone but he was in the opposite gang. All I heard was yelling. "My God, he was shot!" I can still hear her scream to this day. He dropped to the ground while still holding her hand. I started to run down the stairs and went outside. I saw his brain was scattered all over the sidewalk.

It happened so fast I remember I couldn't move. A car pulled up. Someone yelled at me, "Get in the fucking car." I was grabbed by my shirt and thrown in a car. I thought to myself, *what is going on?*

My heart was racing. Everyone started running.

Now we were fighting everywhere. There were shootings and deaths all because of the colors I decided to represent. I saw beatdowns, more blood, and people being hospitalized.

I remember one incident that would change my view and force me to make changes. This was when they terminated my brother, my real blood brother. They beat him so badly that when he arrived to my place all I could do was cry. His face was so swollen and there was blood all over. Rage took over. I wanted to kill them for doing that to my brother. In my head, I was like, this can't be my life. What the fuck? The next morning I wanted to go after the ones who were responsible. I didn't care if I died in the process.

I was in the middle of the street screaming, "Fuck you, come hit me. I got something for ya."

I can hear some of the guys saying, "Daisy please stop. It's going to be OK!" But I knew it wouldn't be...

I thought to myself, *what is next?* I became so numb. I didn't even cry anymore. The police were trying to stop it and were not succeeding. We had marches that I participated in up and down Park Street. We would get sprayed in the face by police officers and detained. The police were all over us. They played no games. My God! I couldn't breathe, choking and screaming, "I can't see." I became fed up with this so-called life I chose.

The man I loved was so wrapped up in this life. I felt that it tore us apart. I felt lost. I decided to leave. I wanted more; this could not be what life was all about.

In my head, I was thinking, *what the fuck am I doing with my life?*

11

Choosing My Real Family

I then decided I had to make a choice: keep gang-banging or be a mother to my sons. My sons did not deserve this life I was living. I decided to leave and start my life over again no matter the consequences. This also meant having to move back with my mother. I couldn't tell her anything so my brother and I kept that secret from her.

I remember being in front of my grandmother's house and the girls from the gang told me they had been looking for me and they were going to jump me. I told them I was not afraid and didn't give a fuck. They looked at me and for some reason they said, "Another time," and walked away. So many other times I saw them but I believe it was GOD who protected me.

I had nightmares for years.

Mom had no clue what life I was living. No matter what I did it felt like it was never good enough. Moving in with two children that my mom didn't want to deal with made it worse. It didn't last long. Maybe a couple of months and she had already kicked me out.

It was nothing new. She had been doing this to me for as long as I could remember. By the time I was 15 when we argued or she felt like it got too hard for her, she would say, "Get the fuck out." There was no communication with my mother, just yelling and then she would not speak to me for months at times.

I had nothing to fall back on and didn't know what to do next. I had several evictions. I couldn't afford shit and had no support once again. So I had to call one of my aunts and I went to her house. I will never forget my Grandmother Isabel showing up. As she cried with me she stated, "I didn't raise my kids this way. You need help and you are coming with me."

She told me to get my things and my children and she took me home with her. She showed me what unconditional love was. She never judged me! She was tough, though. She didn't take my shit, but she taught me to be a better mother to my children and to be a better woman.

This wasn't the first time my grandmother had taken me in. I stayed with my grandma on and off during my teenage years. This time I was 20 and I came with two kids but she never complained. She definitely saved my life. I loved her more than life itself. She taught me how to save my money and have things in my life of importance. She definitely was strict and things had to be spotless. My grandmother helped me by saving the money I received from welfare. This helped me get my own place.

I was able to find a new place a block over from where she lived. I was finally happy. I had a one-bedroom apartment. My boys had the bedroom and I slept in the living room. I still had a lot of growing up to do. Again, with no job and being on welfare, I was thinking, *how in the hell am I going to do this?* I hadn't finished high school. I couldn't think clearly about what my future would even look like.

12

Together at Gunpoint

During this time I met a man that one of my cousins introduced me to. Boy was he fine. This was during the summer of 1994. My life would all change. I was sitting on my grandmother's porch with my cousin. He came over to say hi. We talked a little.

It was broad daylight when two guys came up to us. One was a young Black kid and the other was a Puerto Rican kid. Both had guns. I remember looking up and saying, "Holy shit."

The crazy part was they wanted to just rob us. He made the two guys we were talking to lay on the cement. One of them took his jacket off and laid it on the floor before going down on his stomach. My life just flashed in front of me. I thought I was going to die! As these two assholes waved their guns (one had a TEC-9 and the other a Glock.) They robbed us and threatened to kill us.

We went through all of that for jerks to only get seven dollars in cash and a damn beeper. I was thinking to myself, "I'm not giving them shit." I put my hands in my pocket because I had jewelry on and my cousin put her face in my chest as she was so afraid. He screamed at me, "Stop fucking looking at me!" but I couldn't help it. He taunted us with the gun as if he was going to shoot us. Then they both ran off.

We were so angry. People saw this happening from their windows and weren't sure what they were looking at. The mom of one of the guys who was robbed came flying up the street in her car. She said, "What the hell is going on?" We told her. She went and got us a shotgun. We sat on the porch and said, "If these mother fuckers come back we are shooting them." Of course, I was okay with that since they almost took our life. We hung out until two in the morning to see if they would come back. But they never did.

Even with all that I decided to stay for about a week with my grandmother since my kids were with their father for the week. The new guy and I were hanging out and getting to know each other more. It just got more insane. I was walking to the burger place and was told, "When I say run I mean run." Well, shit I did. All I heard were shots being let off. My cousin and I ran up the stairs of a building and hid for a few and then ran back to my grandmother's house. We heard footsteps behind us when we looked we saw one of our friends get pistol-whipped over and over again. They finally stopped and ran off and we had to call 911. Our friend was bleeding and having a seizure. We knew he was going to be hospitalized. He was never the same.

These random shootings and fights continued for about a week. I then decided it was time for me to leave my grandmother's house and go gack to my own place where I thought there would be less chaos!

The guy and I continued talking and seeing each other. Not even three months later, we moved in together and got a new apartment where we began a new life together.

That's when it all started!

He never had an issue with me having two kids as he did not have any.

I thought he was going to be good for me

He charmed me; he was handsome and shy. But he was also temperamental and would fight at the drop of a dime. I looked at him as my protector. I thought he would never do that to me.

Our life began. It was exciting, hard, and confusing but I was in love and I wanted it to work. The signs were all there but I always thought, *It will get better. He will change!*

I never paid attention to the signs! I even saw him choking some chick in the middle of the street saying, "Somebody better come get this bitch!"

I convinced myself that it wasn't his fault.

We argued a lot but he always convinced me that he was sorry and that he loved me. In our first fight he threw a juice container at me, bruising me and threatening me that he would fuck me up. I grabbed a knife and went to stab him to defend myself. He put his arm across his chest, so I ended up stabbing his forearm. His anger was uncontrollable. I called my mom worried, but I wasn't going to take his shit either. I did not know what he was going to do next. My mom arrived in the parking lot but I begged her not to come in. I felt it would make it worse, so I asked her to leave and she did. I tried to calm him down.

I decided to go out one night with my cousin. He wasn't very happy, but I went out anyway. When I arrived at my cousin's house after to drop her off, he was there waiting for us to pull in. He jumped out of the car, opened my door, and punched me dead in the face. In my mind I was saying to myself, *Why did he do that? Why is he so angry?* He then grabbed me and forced me into the car where he had my children in the back seat. He then proceeded to drive the car. He threatened to crash the car into a pole to kill me and my children. I cried and begged him to stop. He just talked shit and finally took us home. I put my children to bed and prayed he wouldn't hit me anymore. I went to my bed and said nothing and waited for him to fall asleep.

In the midst of this, at the age of 26, I was diagnosed with psoriatic arthritis. The pain was indescribable. In the middle of many nights, I would wake up screaming and crying from the pain. I would have to get help in and out of the tub to soak with Epsom salt. Even with this pain, I realized I still had to keep going. I still had to be a mother and still had to keep working. I had to push through, because I felt like if I didn't, what would I have? What kind of life would I have had for myself and my children?

So many things were happening, all the signs were there but I thought that was what love was. He showed me a little at a time. I didn't think anything of it as we were still learning who we were with each other. I should've walked away but I didn't. He asked me to marry him and I said yes. We went through so much, but I still continued with planning our wedding. During my planning, I decided to have all my sisters and brothers in it, since my dad wouldn't be able to be there.

We dated and got married after four years, and bought our first car and our home.

Then it became worse. He was the same man who bought me everything from clothes to jewelry and cars but that came with a price: my happiness, my friends, my family! Slowly he took them away from me! The more I did for myself like school, the better job I had, the worse it would get. He would make comments like, "I know you're going to leave me for someone better or smarter." He would ask why I had to go to school and how I had gotten positions in different jobs. We were the opposite. I was social and happy and loved to help others. He was introverted, judgemental, and controlling. He was happy as long as I did what he wanted.

This became a pattern that would last for the next 22 years.

13

Out of Nowhere

Imagine this.

You hire a landscaper.

He works for you for four years.

And then you find out he murdered seven women!

I could have been his next victim!

He would come every two weeks. He was very kind, always saying hi to my children.

I had no idea what type of monster he was.

He would drive up in his white van and have all his equipment ready for work.

He did a great job! We would pay him 25 dollars and you couldn't beat that!

One day out of the blue he pulled up and said, "I need to talk to you."

I said, "OK."

He came over and told me, "I have to go to Virginia. I don't know when I'm coming back.

I didn't know what to say. I thought it was about a personal matter.

He said he would contact me when he got back.

Later, I was home watching the news and I couldn't believe what I saw and heard.

Our landscaper was wanted for these murders! They caught him in Virginia in the white van he used for working on our lawn. It was the van he used to kill some of his victims.

They found DNA and traces of blood in it.

All I could think of was, *holy shit, that could have been me!*

I would sometimes think why didn't he choose me? Was he waiting for the right time? My God that was so scary. I was confused, scared, and shocked. He could have killed me! He was caught before that happened.

I had successfully survived violence from outside our home. But the violence inside our home was getting worse and worse. And as if that wasn't enough, I was about to lose the most important person in my life.

14

Abuela Isabel

On the first day of summer in 2007, it was raining. Then a burst of sun came out.

When I received the call from my mother that my Abuela was gone I was in disbelief. She said, "I think something is wrong." I told her, "I'm on the way to your house." When I arrived my mom was crying and hysterical. She told me to call my uncle in Puerto Rico. I called and we told him to check on my grandmother. When he arrived he had to break in, only to find her lifeless on her bed. He then told us she was gone. I then had to call all of my family members and tell them the news.

What was I going to do without her? She would call me every Sunday to check up on me and my children. It hurt me so much that she was at home alone when she passed. Our family decided to bring her back to Connecticut for her burial. We met at the funeral home to set up the day and time. Seeing her in the casket crushed me. I was still in denial. She looked so beautiful. I went to kiss her on her cheek. She was still so soft but she was so cold. I could hear everyone talking and people crying.

I just wanted it to be a dream.

I went outside. I couldn't breathe. When they walked outside carrying her casket I fainted in my cousin's arms. My other grandmother Maria grabbed me. She wiped my tears and said, "Don't cry, she is in a better place." I told myself I would never want to visit her at the cemetery because that was not how I wanted to remember her. It's her voice, her love, and her direction in my life that I miss the most, and I wanted to remember that.

When my grandmother died the glue that tied our family together was missing. We all fell apart.

Later the nine cousins became eight when one of my cousins died. I thank God my grandmother didn't have to bury her grandchild. I don't think she would have been able to handle that type of pain.

I was home when I heard a bang on the door early in the morning that scared me. I ran to the door to see who it was. It was Tony, my cousin who I considered my brother.

I looked at his face I knew something was wrong, "What is it?" I asked.

He started crying and fell to his knees and said, "Evelyn is gone."

I was confused and asked, "What are you talking about?"

He told me she died in a car accident. We cried together. I just couldn't understand. How could this have happened? A drunk driver going 100 mph the wrong way on the highway had hit her. We talked and decided to all meet at his mom's house later that day.

It was never the same after but we all were very supportive. We were all living our separate lives but up until then we always made sure that we checked on each other and made sure we were all doing ok. As for my life, I was just trying to survive my own hell.

15

Devil in Disguise

My husband began to physically abuse me more often. I had left one nightmare to begin another one.

One night, I decided to go out with my friends from work. We went to a happy hour. My God, it was fun but I knew when I got home there would be some shit. I did drink a little too much. I was in the bathroom peeing and vomiting in the bathtub. It was a little rough. He was so pissed at me, not because of the drinking but because I went out. He got some hot water and threw it on me. Then he told me to get in the damn shower. I could barely stand. Finally, I was able to go and lay down. I forced myself to sleep. I knew in the morning there was going to be more shit from him. After a while, there was just silence.

We didn't speak for days. Nothing new.

It was a cold day in December, almost Christmas. I was so excited for the kids and for them to open all of their gifts. He walked in the house in one of his moods. We had a disagreement that led to arguing and yelling. He decided to take the Christmas tree and throw it to the ground in the living room, breaking a lot of the ornaments. I was thinking, *Here we go again.* The tears were rolling down my face. I was asking *why do I stay?* He then took all the gifts and put them in his car and said no one was getting shit.

I yelled, "What do the kids have to do with it?"

But I realized a long time ago he does it because he knows that would hurt me more. I hated him!

I remember praying that he would just leave.

Finally, he left. The kids came down from their rooms. The looks on their faces filled with pain. I told them it was going to be ok. My daughter wiped the tears from my face and said, "Mommy, it's going to be ok" as I picked up the broken ornaments from the floor. I put the tree back and cleaned up.

That night we did not say a word to each other. A couple of days later he brought the gifts back and said he was sorry. I didn't believe him. But I told him, "OK," so that my kids would have a good Christmas.

There was a Christmas party I went to for a job where my cousin and I worked. We went to the gathering in a ballroom at a hotel. I was coming out of a room with my husband and DMX was there. He walked by me and stopped and looked at me and said, "Hello." I said, "Hi," back. I couldn't believe I met him.

He then said, "Hey, after my concert there is an after-party you should come."

I said, "Thank you but I can't."

He walked away with a smile. My husband was so angry. He started yelling at me and called me a fucking groupie. He said, "We are going home."

I told him, "Absolutely not. We are here for the Christmas party and I'm not leaving."

I walked into the ballroom and started dancing with my cousin and my friends. He grabbed my arm, "Let's go."

I said, "No."

He then walked off and left me there but I knew my cousin would take me home. I knew when I got home there was going to be a fight. At this point, I didn't give a shit anymore.

Another time he had a small safe with a key that I was not allowed to have. He decided to open it one night. I was standing in the kitchen while he sat at the dining room table with the kids. I happened to look over and saw money and pictures. I asked, "What the hell is that?"

He closed it quickly and said, "Nothing." I demanded to see it. He said, "It's not what you think." He opened it and there were nude pictures of other women. He claimed that he was working on a calendar and they were posing for it and that is how he was making extra money by selling the calendars. I didn't believe him. He yelled at me and said I was doing too much. He took the pictures and had thousands of dollars in cash and put it in our fireplace and lit it and burned everything and looked at me and said, "It doesn't mean shit to me."

As much as it hurt, he manipulated me into believing he loved me and that he was sorry. I knew in my mind this was just another lie, but I stayed because I was always afraid he would make it worse than it already was.

Every summer we had cookouts and pool parties. I loved to have them. Family and friends were always invited. At one of the family gatherings, we were having a great time until he and my brother had an argument. I asked my brother to please leave but he had been drinking and was arguing with him. I told him to ignore my brother and to please go into the house. My kids and all their friends ran into the house. They watched from our dining room window, not knowing what was going on.

I got in the middle of him and my brother. Before we knew it he punched my brother and knocked him out. My mother yelled so loud with fear in her voice. I was so angry. He then just walked away towards the house. I helped my brother up and told him to leave. All the kids were in disbelief. I told them everything was going to be OK and continued to play.

He destroyed our get-together and didn't care who he was going to hurt.

I felt he couldn't control my life so he tried to destroy my happiness and hurt me in all ways possible.

Getting punched in the face, slapped, choked out, and threatened with a baseball bat, a knife put in our wall while he stared at me in our bed, saying "If you ever leave..." These were the things I was going through. But I was too afraid to leave!

He would come into the house and start destroying it. Glass tables being smashed to pieces. Our glass top stove being broken by the force of his fist. Breaking things in the garage including the walls. I feel like he wanted to make me feel that I would have nothing if I went against him

I am very vocal, especially now. He didn't like me to have a voice towards HIM. For others, he didn't mind. I couldn't have friends do things that didn't involve him in it. When I did I would come home to consequences.

We decided to take a trip to Virginia Beach with the children. I knew it wasn't a good idea. I knew that it could be bad at any time with him.

We went and played miniature golf, played football on the beach, and went shopping in different stores. We let the kids get whatever they wanted. We even went on a speedboat where we witnessed a dead body in the underpath. See, working in the hospital for as long as I had, I knew what death looked like even from a distance. I made the workers call the ambulance and it confirmed exactly what I thought. We actually got off the boat and into our van and drove to where the body was because my kids wanted to see it up close. I'm like, "Oh my God, okay."

So we went. My daughter yelled at her brother, "You better not take any pictures." We then heard the ambulance coming so we all ran back to our van and drove off.

We went on with our trip. They were long and fun days there. But of course one of the nights he decided to start an argument about my phone. He said that he was going to take the rental car and leave us there and that we would have to find a way home. Mind you, we were 10 hours away from home. He left the room and I didn't know what to do. This was mentally draining. My kids were so upset I told them I would figure it out and not to worry. Several hours later he came back and I had to beg him to stay so that we wouldn't be stranded. I hated him for this but this was how he got his way.

All of my children played sports and I never missed any practice or any of their games. One day, we were all on our way to watch Schamar play football in Massachusetts. It was cloudy that day, the sun would peak in and out. The air smelled like wet grass.

I had some family members come out to support and cheer him on. I sat on the metal bench. It was so uncomfortable so I moved to my beach chair. While I watched my son run up and down the field, I would cheer and yell to let him know I was paying attention.

My phone rang. It was my sister-in-law. We were talking and laughing. My husband didn't like the conversation so he grabbed my hand and tried to grab the phone. I held onto it. He pushed me to the ground, grabbed my phone, and threw it. My phone broke. I started crying and asking, "What are you doing?" He told me to shut up!

A family member came running over and helped me up from the ground. It was humiliating! Everyone knew how he was. They watched and did nothing. My little cousin, a teenager at the time, came running, looked at me, and said, "I won't let him hurt you." I cried. I just thought to myself, *damn, why is this my life?* I told him I was fine and continued the rest of the day as if nothing happened because I didn't want to ruin my son's day. Finally, the game was over. We got in the cars. Everyone then asked if I needed a ride. He looked at me so I said, "No, I'm fine." We drove home in silence.

Another time he came in a bad mood and started arguing with me. My heart dropped. I was alone in the house with him. I started crying and thinking *I gotta get out of here.* He started throwing shit and he went into the bedroom at that moment.

I decided to run out the front door and ran to my neighbor's house and told her that he was going to hurt me. She said, "Over my dead body." She got her shotgun and looked at me and said, "I will use it on his ass if I have to. I will not let him hurt you."

She went outside and told him not to even think of coming onto her property. She then called the cops and told them that she heard him all the time yelling at me and threatening me in front of the kids. By the time they had arrived, he took off and they put out a warrant for his arrest. The officer called him on his phone and let him know he had to turn himself in. Several hours later, he did. They contacted me to let me know that he was in their custody. It didn't last long. He was back at the house the next morning.

The fighting and arguing were ridiculous and I didn't know how to get out and fix my life for me and my kids. As soon as he started his shit again the kids would be afraid. We would run out of the house and pray he would stop. His mother had been there witnessing some of these events. She couldn't stop him. She would never do anything and never wanted us to call the police on him. I would be afraid to call the cops because of what he would do to me after.

The kids started to get fed up and started calling the cops on him. My youngest was to me the bravest of us all. I should have been able to leave and take them with me so that they didn't have to see so much. Schamar had to witness his father choke me out, slap me, threaten me, and break shit. But he got fed up and started to call the cops on his father.

His father would tell him, "When the cops get here you tell them that I didn't do anything and that you called by accident."

Schamar would say, "No, I'm going to tell them the truth."

From the age of 12 to 16 he had to grow up fast. He had already witnessed this shit all his life but it had gotten worse. He stood up to his father and looked at him and stated "I am not scared of you. You are not going to hurt my mom." See his other brothers went off to college and the other one moved out and his sister was afraid to say anything. She would lock herself in her room. But do you blame them? I don't. I blame myself!

Every get-together I had he made sure to destroy it. I had a birthday get-together at the casino. Family and friends came out. He started an argument. He took my money out of my purse and took my car keys. I didn't even know why he did that to me. He started to yell and made a scene in front of everyone. I yelled back. Security came.

He decided to walk away but what I didn't know was he left with my car so I had to have my friends bring me home.

The worst part was he kept calling me to say that he got in an accident and was in a ditch so I found the state police in the casino. I was crying and afraid. They told me that there were no accidents reported. They couldn't find him anywhere so we got in the car and decided to try and find him and couldn't.

He then called again and told my older son he was lost and cold and in a ditch and needed help. But he couldn't tell us where he was but why would he keep calling us and not the police? We were all really exhausted and decided to go home.

We finally made it home at 6 am to find that he was there the whole time. Our damn car was parked in the driveway. He had lied. He never got into a car accident at all.

I walked into our home. He was lying on the couch like nothing ever happened. He stood up and started arguing again. He hit me. I fell to the couch. I yelled, "What the fuck are you doing? Why did you lie? What are you hitting me for? Where are my kids?"

He said they were sleeping. I was confused because I had left my kids with my cousin. I was so angry, embarrassed, tired, and just fed up.

16

The Things My Son Witnessed

My youngest kids heard me screaming and crying. He had slapped me to the floor. He then pulled out a metal bat and banged it on the floor twice and told me he was going to hit me with it. The kids were afraid and they decided to call the police. My youngest came running up the stairs to my bedroom and pushed the door open and said, "I called the police on you!" His father told him to tell the police he called in error. My son said, "No, I will not lie. You hit my mom!"

When the officers arrived, he tried to tell the officers that I had been writing to another man. I literally showed them the letters he had been writing and the paperwork that I had to show that it was not my handwriting. He had been doing this for months and arguing with me and it was all his doing. I couldn't even tell you why he did this. The officer then handcuffed him and arrested him. He just wanted control and I felt he wanted to isolate me from everyone he could.

He would start showing up where I worked at the hospital, he would make me miserable with his insecurities. He would come to my office and throw his wedding ring at me to tell me he had divorce papers for me. I couldn't say hi to anyone that he felt threatened by.

I worked with a lot of great people. They never knew what I was going through.

We had a coworker that we all considered a friend. Unfortunately, he was arrested. We had no information on why. So everyone in our unit decided to write to him and make sure he was ok.

This is the twist. I wrote to him as a group and this young man decided to write back to all of us individually. I received the letter which he decided to open and read. He then told me that I was not allowed to write to this young man so I never wrote to him again because I wanted to avoid conflict. But my husband decided to write back to him without telling me and pretended it was me.

He also had a female friend of his pretend she was me and would write to my friend while he was locked up. He would check the mailbox every day until he got a response. Then he'd blame me when I would say I didn't know why I was receiving a letter. He would call me a liar. "How am I a liar?" I asked. He would start yelling and then hit me, knowing the whole time he was doing that shit himself.

We had a mutual friend who would come over all the time to do music with him. On this day the gentleman could not reach him so he just showed up at the house. He asked me if he could go downstairs with my sons and work on some music until he got home from work. I said yes. I thought nothing of it. When he arrived I told him his friend was downstairs. He started arguing with me asking, "Why the fuck is he here?"

I told him to calm down but he wouldn't listen. He went downstairs and told his friend to leave. At that moment I decided to lock myself in the bathroom with my son. I started praying he would calm down and stop yelling. I started giving my son a bath when he busted in and started choking me in front of my son.

What I will never forget was my son yelling, "Please stop!" and crying until I passed out.

I never understood why he was mad and why he attacked me. He just told me that I better ask him first before I let him in. I locked myself in my room wishing someone would come save me.

One day I came home from work at Hartford Hospital and picked up my two younger children. When I pulled up, he was in front of the house yelling, "The devil lives here!"

He drew a demon on my steps. I was so afraid.

My kids didn't understand why. I told the kids, "I promise I won't let him hurt you!"

We took off. I took them for a ride hoping when we got back he would be gone. Well, he was, so we ran into the house. The kids got the things that were important to them. I packed some clothes for all of us. The only place we could go at the time was my mom's house. I thought he was going to hurt me again!

When things like this would happen we would stay at my mom's for a couple of days. He would call me over and over again. We would catch him driving by my mom's house for days but he never messed with my mom. She would never come to her door. He kept calling until I answered and then he would convince me that he was sorry again and that he loved me. He told me it was going to be different and that he wanted his family back.

PEOPLE this was not LOVE but MANIPULATION, FEAR, and CONTROL that he had over me. This went on for years until I started to stand up for myself and thought, *fuck this I'm leaving.* I could face dying while trying to leave. That was better than dying from staying in this so-called marriage.

I told him I had enough. I was leaving and I wanted a divorce. He decided to call my brother one day and tell him that he swallowed pills and wanted to kill himself. Of course, I didn't know so when he arrived worried I asked him why he was at my home. When my brother told me I was furious. I felt he did this just so that I would feel guilty and stay with him. I knew he was full of shit. He just wanted attention and wanted me to feel sorry for him. Well, I didn't!

17

Chaos

Working at Hartford Hospital was the most gratifying job I ever had. I was able to help people every day. People would always ask, "Why do you work in the ER? That place is crazy! So many deaths!" My answer was, "There is also a lot of life."

Working there made me appreciate life and look at things from a different perspective. I saw and heard so many things while being part of the chaos in the ER. There was never a dull moment. The calls would come in at all times of the day or night…stabbings, shootings, injuries, suicide attempts, accidents, deaths, attempted murders, heart attacks, broken bones, stillborn babies, and children.

One night, a child came in who wasn't even four. He was unresponsive. They did everything to try to revive him. He didn't make it. I can still see the mother's face. I can hear the scream as she fell to the floor begging them to help her son. She was not comprehending that they did everything they could.

A husband and wife came in. She was pregnant, bleeding and was losing her baby. I held her while she gave birth to a stillborn. I had to translate because she only spoke Spanish. As the nurse grabbed the lifeless baby and just put it in a bucket that I had to label and cover and take away as the father yelled, "I want to keep my baby." I had to tell him that the baby didn't make it and we had to save his wife who was bleeding out.

There was a woman who had a heart attack and died for about 45 minutes. They fought for her to come back and didn't give up. We witnessed the monitor showing a heartbeat. It was so amazing. She was alive. They saved her!

So many lives were saved day in and day out. There was never a dull moment there.

One gratifying moment I encountered was when an older man who was discharged. I happened to be walking by and his wife said, "My husband doesn't seem right."

I asked, "Where did you guys come from?

She stated that he was a patient but they were sending him home as they felt he was fine.

He might have been fine in the hospital, but when I looked at him I knew he wasn't fine now. I asked a couple of questions that I have heard a million times for people who may be having a stroke. He didn't know where he was or what year it was and he couldn't tell me who the president was. I yelled for security. They rushed him to the ER. The next day the wife came to find me and thank me for saving her husband's life. I didn't think I did anything but my job.

I think the best part was watching everyone working together and having the same goal and that was to save the patient. It made me come home and appreciate life and my children even more. I wanted to do more so I joined a team that was created to make the hospital better.

There was one time when I had to face something there that I'd never thought I'd have to. I was at work calling in a patient to get her information to be admitted to the hospital. A man was escorting an elderly woman in a wheelchair into my office.

As I looked up to greet them I realized it was him—the boy that said I could trust him, the boy at the back of the school who tried to rape me.

My stomach dropped and suddenly I felt nauseous. "What information do you need?" he asked.

I couldn't even find the words to respond to him. I was speechless and terrified.

A woman who I worked with noticed the blank expression on my face, so she called me over the phone to avoid confusion with the patients. She asked if I was okay. I responded with, "No."

She asked if I would like for her to take over the patients. I said very calmly, "Yes."

I walked out of the room and excused myself while my co-worker took over. I waited until they left, hoping I would never see him again. It was crazy how he acted as if he never tried to rape me. As if he didn't know who I was.

18

Mugshot

On my way to work at Hartford Hospital one cold morning, we started arguing in the car. He wanted to know if I was talking to other men on my phone. I said, "What are you talking about?" He starting yelling. I told him to take me to work. I yelled, "You're going to make me late."

He told me he wasn't going to let me out of the car. He started speeding and driving recklessly. He then drove toward a pole, then turned the wheel and dodged it. My heart felt like it was coming out of my chest. I begged him to stop and just take me to work. He refused. I screamed and cried. We fought over a cell phone that went on for about 30 minutes. He hit my head on the glass of the car door and told me he wasn't going to let me out. He then finally drove to my job and told me to get out! I went into work a mess and my eyes were swollen from all the crying. My supervisor asked me what was wrong so I told her. My supervisor put an alert out not to let him in the building if he showed up. A while later an officer showed up but not because I called!

My husband had called the police and lied and told them that I put my hands on him.

The crazy part was the police showed up at my job to arrest me. The officer called him to see if he was sure that he wanted to press those charges. He gave him about 10 chances to say something. He kept repeating, "Well, I have to think about it."

The officer said, "Sir this is your wife."

He didn't care. It was his word against mine! I was so embarrassed. The officer said, "Sorry, but I have to take you in."

The security said, "Please walk her out without cuffs and let her meet you a block away so no one would know what was going on at work." The officer agreed. He then handcuffed me and put me in the back of the cruiser.

I arrived at the precinct. They took my fingerprints and my mugshot. All I could do was cry.

The Lieutenant saw me. "Daisy is that you? Why are you here?"

I spoke to him and explained the situation, as we knew each other. The cop who arrested me said, "I didn't know you knew her!" I told him no one was listening to me.

He said, "Get her out of there."

By this time, the bastard had shown up at the police station saying that he was worried about me and wanted to know if I was ok. The officer then questioned my husband and the tables had turned. Now he was being arrested for kidnapping and forcing me to stay in the car and threatening my life!

Many have asked why I stayed with him. My answer: FEAR is why!

I went home and was there for several hours. He was then bonded out and all hell broke loose. He blamed me for everything. Then he said he was sorry and he was going to change. I was afraid and decided to help him find an attorney so that he wouldn't lose his job. I wanted a divorce so bad but I was afraid of what he would do to me.

I never wanted to let people know when I needed help because I felt that my issues were not theirs. I felt I could figure it out because that is something I had to do all my life.

19

Feeling Hopeless

In May 2014 I had to leave my job and never work again per my doctor. I had always been sick and knew this day would come eventually. I gave my notice at work and called my husband and told him. He didn't say too much for a while. Then in a month or so, his reaction was, "Well who the fuck is going to help with everything?" Mind you, he made plenty of money. I had to drain my entire 401k to pay bills and buy shit for the house and buy everything my kids needed. In November I applied for social security which I got approved for in 30 days. I had been sick since I was 26 and it just got worse with time. I thought he out of everyone would have been more understanding. We weren't struggling so what was the fucking problem?

I finally started to receive my benefits and I was able to continue to take care of my part of the bills. I was less stressed but shit never changed. At the end of this same year, I had to get a total hip replacement. They said it would be months before

I recovered. I was determined to get my life back to normal whatever that was.

I had just got home. I was using a walker to get around and I had to feed my family. So with that walker, I got myself to the kitchen and started cooking. He never helped, he just started arguing with me again. He was looking for an excuse to leave the house I guess! I was so fed up so I grabbed a knife and held it while I cooked. I told him to leave me the fuck alone. He said, "Or what the fuck are you going to do?" He knew I couldn't do much.

My youngest stood right next to me and said, "Don't say anything, just ignore him."

I couldn't though. I wanted to show him I was tough enough and I wasn't going to take his shit!

He eventually walked out of the house. I hated him so much. At this point, I knew I had to get better sooner than later. I took no pain meds and in three weeks with a nurse and therapy, I was walking without assistance. Then I started planning how I was going to get out of this marriage. I was done.

It was getting worse at home. Not only my children tried to help me. One of my boy's friends that I considered one of my sons came to visit. He happened to witness and hear my husband tell me that I wasn't shit. He became more vulgar and said, "Go out and suck some dicks, and just get the fuck out of the house."

I cried because I was embarrassed. I told him to shut up. He wouldn't. He then told my son's friend James to leave the house. James looked at me crying and said to him, "I'm not going anywhere."

I will never forget how he stood up for me. He was a young boy himself at the time.

My husband finally walked out of the house. I knew he would be back later. It wasn't over.

20

Fear is a Mother Fucker

How can a man that you loved for 22 years continue to rip your fuckin' soul out of your body and hurt you over and over and over?

I wanted my life back. My LIFE!

When arguments occurred they escalated very quickly. I couldn't express if I didn't like something or didn't agree because if I did he would become angry. He always stated that it was my fault because I made him upset. He would always say, "If you don't do A and B then I wouldn't hit you or break things." So many years my kids and I had to endure this shit.

He was good at MANIPULATION!

I swear it was always something. I didn't know when it was going to happen.

By 2012 I lost control of what we called a marriage. I started calling the police. My God, so many times he went to jail and they let him come right back.

I was then getting arrested because it didn't matter who started it, we both had to go.

There were so many times the officers would come to our home that they would take him and give me a promise to appear because they knew I had to stay with my kids.

I believe he waited until my older boys left home for him to become worse.

I know he wanted me to be put out of the house so he could stay there with the younger two. DCF was involved on several occasions and they found that his stories never added up and the kids were older so they were able to be interviewed. So he was exposed even more. They dropped the cases within 10 days on one occasion.

He went as far as having one of his family members lie in court for him just to have my kids taken away. They gave him temporary custody of my son but because he was 16 he didn't have to go with him and my son refused to go and the police said he didn't have to. He would never want to leave me.

Behind the lies, I almost lost everything. I was in jail, court, anger management, community service, and the whole time I was just trying to protect myself.

These numbers were a part of my life since the beginning of our relationship.

DOCKET NUMBERS
H14HCR120663317S
HHDFA164084301S
H14HCR12663315
H12MCR160258079S
166068756

CASE NUMBERS
11242016
201500032296
201200028697
201000035564
201600031046
1631017
201500027894
201400027868
201100033475
These are just a few.

Life, I must say, isn't easy for anyone but, when you live with someone who is controlling, and abusive physically and verbally, YOUR WORLD WILL BE TURNED UPSIDE DOWN.

The question is, how do you get your life back? You ask, how it is YOUR own LIFE when you are living in fear?

He had me convinced that what he did, he did out of LOVE. Well, I guess I had to learn that I was not loving myself enough to know that what he had for me was NOT LOVE!

See everyone has opinions on what they would have done but trust me, no one can tell you how or what they would've done if they have never lived in your shoes.

I say it took me 22 years to finally realize I had had enough and it was time to stand and fight back. See, I believed that he would have killed me if I left him.

I decided to leave, even though it was at the worst point in my life. I was so sick. My psoriatic arthritis was so chronic I couldn't do anything for myself. The pain was the worst ever! I was in and out of the doctor's office and hospital. The medications were not working! The meds had me vomiting and created palpitations, I thought and felt like I was not going to make it.

There were so many stories of domestic violence where I would hear, "HE murdered her." I saw and witnessed so much of this while working in the emergency room. I just needed courage and a plan.

When I left I was still afraid for a while. I never knew what he was going to do next or if he would show up out of nowhere.

Then it hit close to someone I knew personally. I knew of a woman in the same situation married with four children and everyone told her to leave. She stayed and she paid with her life. You see he killed her and one of their children who tried to protect her and then he killed himself. I had no words and I promised myself I would never let anyone hurt me or my children ever again.

21

Unbearable

Boy was I afraid but I had had enough.

I wanted to live my own life so I did it. In 2016, I served him the divorce papers. We were still living together. He wouldn't leave and started arguments with me. The police would be at the house every other day. The officers knew us very well and I begged the courts to get him out of the house while we were going through the divorce. It took forever. Finally, the courts had him leave as I feared for my life.

He came after me mentally to break me and to tear my family apart. He wrote poems attacking me on social media. I found out he was having an affair and had another child I had never known about.

He would drive by every day and sit there and watch us and the house at all different times of the day and night. There was nothing I could do. I never slept. I knew I had to keep going. A trial was going to begin as he refused to agree to mediation. He would fight everything. Most of the time he didn't even show up.

I was trying to figure out how in the hell I was going to afford my lawyer. I was already receiving letters for my mortgage being behind. I still had to pay my bills, feed my children, and deal with my sickness. I just wanted it to be a nightmare that I would wake up from. I cried, screamed, and wanted to give up but I knew I couldn't do that. So I tried to mentally prepare myself for what was coming.

Going to court over and over again was draining and mentally exhausting. Imagine sitting there and just hearing the man you once loved tell lies and try to destroy your life little by little. I just wanted the house for a place for my children. He said he would make sure I felt what it was to have nothing if I wouldn't stay with him. I told myself that I couldn't give up and I had to stay strong for myself and my kids. He was killing me piece by piece.

There was nothing I could have done but go through it all and try to prove I wasn't the problem. The officer knew when I called what they were up against. It took me years of asking the court to have him leave the home for our safety. While in court during the divorce proceedings in 2016 I requested a protective order and for him to vacate the home. It was finally granted on January 2, 2017.

Time after time the kids would ask, "How is everything?" I would say, "It's fine, I got this. We are going to be ok."

I remember coming home after court one time. I walked in and my daughter asked, "Are you ok?" This time, I fell to my knees and broke. She went right on the floor on her knees and held me and said, "Everything is going to be ok." I said, "I don't think I can do this anymore."

As a mom I never wanted to let my children see me break but how much can one person take?

He made this part of his life to make me suffer. He told his mother that she was not allowed to see her grandkids and told his family that they could not speak to me.

I felt defeated. It was 2017 and 2018. I was still going and I was still fighting.

I finally got the house, but we were three years behind on payments that he was obligated to pay and never did, so the house went into foreclosure. He made sure I lost it!

In 2019 there were fewer court dates since everything was finally almost all settled.

I tried everything until I felt I was done fighting. He stopped paying the credit cards. They were all in our names and this destroyed my credit. I had to find a place to live with my youngest son. At any time the courts could tell me I had 60 days to get out of the house. This was the worst feeling in the world. I felt like I won even after losing everything because I still had my children and myself.

Everything else didn't matter. The house, the car, the credit cards, these were all replaceable.

I think the most disgusting thing was going through court and being lied to and lied about. He was telling everyone that I wasn't a good mother. He was determined to take my youngest from me. He had me arrested for lies! My daughter was almost arrested after DCF was called on me and my children. He tried to tear us apart but this only made the kids hate him and he blamed me. Little by little they realized he didn't have my children's best interest in mind, it was just to hurt us.

He continued to try to destroy my character with family and friends and made them choose between us. I really didn't care about me but my children were abandoned in the process. The worst part was that people did choose instead of staying neutral and out of our business. No one ever asked our side of the story. I didn't bother to explain or to even prove anything. See, I feel the truth will always come to light and so will the lies.

Life went on and he still continued to have me go to court. Another year went by. I couldn't believe we were going into a new year: 2020.

22

Life Changing

I had been in and out of the hospital for many years. 2020 was the worst of all. In February, I had another flare-up. I couldn't move. I screamed and cried. My son Mike had to undress me and put me in the shower as water usually helped me become mobile. One day, it didn't work so Mike called 911. The ambulance arrived and I was brought to the ER. I was told I couldn't go home and they admitted me and I was there for the next five days.

My doctor couldn't even explain to me what happened or even what to do next. Those five days were insane. There were many meds for pain and inflammation. A lot of family and friends showed up. It was crazy and scary but the amazing support I received was like no other.

Because I had worked in the ER in the past and knew so many people, I ended up having great people who made sure I received the best care.

I was transferred upstairs very smoothly and the care I received was phenomenal. I just wanted the pain to stop. My kids and family and friends were all there making me laugh when I wanted to cry. The process was indescribable. It felt like an eternity but they finally controlled it and five days later I was able to go home. I thought it was going to go back to normal but that didn't happen. A couple of weeks later, in March, I became sick with a simple cold that turned into an upper respiratory infection (metahuman pneumonia). I was told once again I couldn't go home. I was hospitalized again for five days.

This is when the world went insane and COVID-19 was discovered. I couldn't stop coughing. The doctors came in with suits that covered them from head to toe. I couldn't breathe and I didn't want to eat. I was weak and scared. No one had answers.

My kids were not allowed to come and visit me. I decided to make a video explaining to everyone that this COVID shit was serious and for everyone to take care of themselves because being alone and in the hospital is something they didn't want to experience. I posted this all over social media. They had so many questions that I couldn't answer because the hospital didn't have any answers. I would look out the window and see so many people coming in. Then I noticed they were putting tents and stations for people to be seen instead of letting them into the hospital. They then tested me and I was told it could take more than seven days. They decided to send me home on the fifth day with no results. They told me to stay in my bedroom and stay away from my kids. I told them, "What kind of shit was that? What if my kids got it?" I was so angry. I went home. Several days later they called to say I was negative. But it didn't end there.

While at home I became worse. I called my doctor. He told me that I couldn't come into the office and that I had to ride it out. He called in something for my cough and a pump to help me breathe. Then I had a fever and my body ached. I called again and told him there was something wrong. He said unfortunately I have to feel like I'm almost dying for him to send me to the ER. I then said, "I feel like I am dying. I can't breathe."

He finally told me to go to the ER. When I arrived they were having a damn parade and life stars were flying around. The police, the fire department, and the ambulance all attended!

My son Justin said, "I can't get through." He watched me get worse.

I couldn't take the pain in my chest. We sat in the car for almost an hour. Finally, he got me to the doors of the ER where the tents were out. They took my temperature and rushed me to x-ray my chest. I was told I had full-blown pneumonia. They stated I had viral pneumonia, suspected COVID-19 infection, on top of psoriatic arthritis, and menorrhagia. They told me I was not going home and I was admitted again. I was tested for COVID-19 again and had to wait for the results. I was in so much pain I cried and I had no family because it was not permitted. I was alone again and scared. I thought I was going to die! My chest got tighter. They had to put on an oxygen tank and my heart was beating out of my fucking chest. At this point, my heart was tachycardic at 145bp. I was bleeding from my period that turned into hemorrhaging, and I had no energy. I then started having anxiety attacks that I could not control or stop. *My GOD please help me.* No one knew what to do.

I was very lethargic but in my mind I knew I couldn't DIE. I fought because I needed to be with my children. This continued for days. They then decided to transfer me to Bliss 7 on the fourth day. This was the worst floor ever at the time. So many people had COVID and were very sick. The nurses were overwhelmed. I felt like I did not receive the care that I needed. I couldn't sleep and to make it worse COVID-19 was at its worst and I had to share a room. The hospital was full. One patient decided to be discharged because she was afraid to share a room with anyone as people were dying of COVID-19. They then transferred me to another room with another patient. She was so sweet. She was discharged the next day.

By then I was on my third roommate. She was awful and rude and up all night on her phone. I could not sleep. Not only was I irritated but in pain and having trouble breathing. I was mentally and physically tired. They did so many tests and gave me breathing treatments that made me feel like shit. I had the jitters and was very weak. At this point, I became a bed risk as I couldn't do anything for myself. I couldn't stand or walk without assistance. On many occasions, I was waiting on PCAs to help me. I was frustrated and yelling and peeing on myself. They had to help me to the shower where they had to put a chair in the shower because I was unable to stand. They then decided to get me a therapist to try to help me walk. They had me use a walker because I could only take a couple of steps. The weakness in my legs was bad. They then attached a machine and socks to keep my blood flowing so I wouldn't get blood clots. My heart rate was still tachycardic and the doctor could not figure out why.

I felt more stress being in the hospital environment. I wanted to just go home. The 6th and 7th day they would assist me with a walker. I would take five steps and my heart would be in my throat. I just wanted to get the fuck out of there. On the 8th day, I decided I wanted to leave. The doctor said OK but he made sure that a nurse and a therapist were set up for home visits. During that whole time, no one had answers but my tests kept coming back negative for COVID. I just didn't understand.

My son Justin picked me up and the other boys were home awaiting my arrival. Schamar helped Justin get me out of the car and helped me up the stairs and into my bed. For three whole weeks, I went through therapy and learned how to walk all over again. This was another scary moment but I wasn't giving up. I then had to follow up with a cardiologist and pulmonary doctor to see if I had a lifetime of damage. By the grace of God, I had nothing. My pulmonary doctor looked me in the eyes and stated, "I don't know how you are here and alive. You should be dead! Your recovery is as if nothing ever happened to you." I had four COVID tests done, all negative. He believed they were wrong. I was told that when I was diagnosed with pneumonia I should have been given antibiotics to survive. But they never did because they thought it was COVID.

For the next couple of years, I worked on getting my life back together. During this time, I got a break from court because of COVID. In April 2022 I had my final court date through Zoom and the judge confirmed that I lost everything. I was told to move out and find a place to live. I had 60 days. I never looked back. What it made me realize was that nothing in life is guaranteed. You can have everything one day and nothing the next. I must say I survived both. Building from nothing makes you humble. I'm still trying to put it all together. I can say some days are easier than others.

23

A Different Kind of Pain

August 16, 2021 was one of the worst days of my life and the most painful. I arrived at my son's house to watch my three grandchildren. It had to be around 8:15 a.m.

My phone rang but the call came from Facebook which I thought was weird and when I saw who was calling me puzzled me even more.

It was Ericka's mom Kat. I answered quickly and said, "Hey what's up?"

All I heard was, "SHE IS GONE."

I said, "Who is gone?"

She said, "ERICKA."

I was confused. "What the fuck are you talking about?"

She replied, "It was a car accident. She didn't make it. I've been calling Schamar but he won't answer."

I started crying uncontrollably. I couldn't breathe. I said, "Don't call my son. I will go home and tell him face-to-face and call you later."

I got the kids in my car and I drove to my house. I swear it was the longest drive ever. I called my other children to tell them what was going on. We were just so hurt.

I finally arrived and walked up the stairs. I told the kids to go watch TV. I opened my son's bedroom door slowly as I was trying to get my thoughts together.

He was sleeping. I had to call his name three times. He finally said, "Yeah mom."

I said, "I have to tell you something. ERICKA is gone."

The first thing he said was, "Did she do it to herself?"

I said, "No it was a car accident."

He looked at his phone and said, "No Mom she was calling. Look."

I said, "That's not her, that's her mom."

He called the number hoping I was wrong. Kat picked up. All I heard was, "How?" Just how. We got ourselves together to go over to her house. I dropped the kids off. Schamar went to meet up with the mom to get answers and we decided to meet up a little later.

My son did the bravest and strongest thing I've ever seen a young man do. He helped her mother with all of the arrangements for the funeral. He viewed the body, and the casket and helped her pick out her dress. He knew what Ericka's favorite dress would be. He called the church he attended since he was a child and got a pastor to come and speak.

The day of the wake was the hardest. I couldn't keep myself together. I wanted to be strong for my son but I tell you, he was strong for me and helped me cope.

I felt this type of pain for my father and grandmother when they passed, but with this, I was beyond hurt. I looked at her in her casket. I kept asking God, "WHY? She was only 20! She had so much more to do." I wanted to take all the pain that my son felt and held inside and take it away.

There were so many people there. Her mom was so loving towards my son and made us feel a part of everything. I thank her for that.

I remember my son standing up and reading what he wrote about her and how much he loved her. It just killed me inside. I just wanted to take away his pain. I recall his brothers never leaving his side and Chole and Brian never leaving mine. We stayed at the casket the whole time I didn't want to leave her. I fixed her hair hoping I would wake up from this horrible dream. Her mother showcased her photos with all of us in them including me. I didn't expect this and it warmed my heart. She also had the paintings that Ericka painted.

We all were in disbelief. I remember having to get ready to go to the burial which I was dreading the whole time. I could barely walk. I needed to be escorted to my car, take a couple of breaths, and try to get myself together. The drive there was not long. Her mom sat me with her and Schamar and her other children. It was time to leave and I just couldn't leave her there. I didn't want to leave. I stayed behind for a little longer and then was told I had to go.

After this long painful day it was time to go home, back to reality and this life that we call normal, but it would never be the same. My son worked every day and crazy hours to stay busy. He never talked about it. I tried to bring her up to Schamar and he would keep it short and change the subject. I had nightmares and depression that I could not shake off. Some people understood while others didn't. I was asked by my own mother, "What is your problem? You act like that was your child!"

She was in my life for almost four years. She was another child of mine to me. I feel I should not have to explain that to anyone.

I would sit at her gravesite for hours every day. I didn't know how to put my life and my son's life back together after this. I went to therapy for a while. It helped a little. Then one day I decided to read the texts that she and I had exchanged. There were so many.

I thank God every day for what she wrote to me before becoming my angel. She wrote that she never wanted to disappoint me and that she was going to get help and do better. I told her that she never disappointed me and that I would be there for her whenever she needed me. What no one knew is how she struggled with depression and didn't want to live and my son tried to save her many times. I thought that maybe I didn't do enough or maybe I could have said more than I did but the truth is she tried to save herself and in the end life just caught up with her. Ericka posted one day that Schamar gave her a reason to live. She stated we showed her unconditional love. See I'm writing this story because her last words were that she LOVED me as if I were her other MOM and she said to me you have to finish your book. I promised her I would, so here I am.

Two weeks passed. I had been in my home wanting not to speak to anyone and feeling very depressed. I could not wrap my head around what had happened and had a lot of guilt. I felt that I could have saved her. I watched my son closely. I knew he was broken but wanted to show me that he was ok. I didn't know how to fix it. It was killing me inside. We were all invited to two baby showers on Saturday the 28th of August. I told my boys that I would meet them there. I got dressed and walked slowly to my car.

It was raining so I was driving slowly. I was merging onto the highway when all of a sudden a Caravan going about 80 mph swerved into my lane. I saw everything in slow motion. I remember yelling, "NO NO NO please!" and *boom* she SLAMMED into my driver's side. I ended up losing control and my car spun out of control. I slammed on my brakes and my SUV went over an embankment on the Merritt Parkway. Ericka came to mind and I screamed out loud, "GOD I'm not ready to die yet." I hit my head on the glass of the driver's side door and went unconscious for a minute. I looked up to realize my car was in between two trees. The key was broken in the ignition and my car was totaled. All I could think about were my children.

I then looked over to my driver's door and realized my door was pinned against the tree and I could not get out. A woman opened the passenger door I could hear her say, "Are you ok?"

I replied, "No."

She said, "Don't worry. I saw everything and I called 911."

I remember her shirt because it had a beautiful colorful butterfly on it. She kept saying, "I won't leave you everything is going to be okay."

I asked her to help me find my phone because I needed to call my sons. We scrambled to find my phone. I told Schamar I was in a car accident. He kept asking me to send my location. I was out of it. Finally she helped me send it to him and he showed up.

We couldn't believe it. We had just gone through this with Ericka not even two weeks prior, like what the fuck? My other son Justin showed up right after they told him to get everything he could out of the vehicle and to take pictures and videos. The state police and the fire department showed up. They got me out of my SUV and onto a stretcher. An ambulance took me to the ER. All I could think about was I'd never been in a car accident in my life, why now?

The craziest part is the woman who hit me her name was also ERICKA.

The next six months I couldn't get it together so I decided to go and get therapy. It helped some and it also opened up other wounds from my past.

I think the worst part is having to go to the cemetery to check on her and talk to a tombstone hoping she can still hear me.

I made Ericka a promise that I would never forget her. When I'm going through things I drive there to tell her, wishing she was still here. I find it to be very peaceful. I know my son misses her so much. I think the hardest part is the pain he endures and I wish I could take it away.

24

Being a Mother First

Staying in this marriage definitely created four different perspectives for my children. All four saw different sides of their father. My older ones were able to be out of the house a lot more and were not really around when it got worse. The last two saw so much.

After my divorce, I was blamed for my children not having a relationship with their father but that's on him.

Being a parent is the hardest job but as parents, we don't get to give up! Our kids are always looking for direction in life. We may not have all the answers but we must try to always do our best.

I feel and see a lot of parents give up so easily with their children and say, "I did enough. You figure it out." Yes, we as parents should learn to have boundaries so that our children can do things on their own but we should make sure that when they need help we are there for them.

In my life, I wanted to help as many people as possible even if that meant just listening, showing up, crying, finding a solution, giving money, cooking food, or giving them a place to stay when needed. I wanted to show my children compassion. My kids would bring all their friends to our home and they would all sleep over, eat, and call me "Mama Daisy." That was so gratifying. I wanted my home to be a safe and loving place, especially for kids. Now those kids are adults and they still are a part of my life!

People wonder why I went so hard for my children. I had to learn to also ask them their side because they have the right to state their truth. I protected them with everything in me but that also came with judgment from others that I enabled them. Yes, I understood what that meant later but knowing that I loved them and that I would do anything for them I never wanted that to be a question by them.

I feel that being a MOM is the best gift GOD gave me. I also feel and believe in unconditional love but I feel you have to have a little tough love. See I only knew what tough love felt like and I didn't want my children to feel that for many reasons. I only knew yelling and beatings so I decided I never wanted to hit my children. My yelling, though, I couldn't control and had to work on. It took growing up and trying to have communication with all my children.

No one owes us anything but a parent owes us protection, security, stability, encouragement, love, and structure. Parents should teach their children morals and respect and allow them to express themselves in healthy ways. Obviously, we choose our own path as we become adults but so many parents forget that it's not just about them once they decide to have a child.

Being a child is to be free, having all the emotions like being mad, sad, happy, encouraging, strong, weak, and not worrying about what others feel and think. As we get older, we start to hold these emotions in as if we aren't allowed to have them. Because some people make you feel you're not entitled to those feelings. Insane, though, I think it's more damaging to us!

Being a mother was and is very important to me. I need and want them to know that I love them unconditionally but I never did this with boundaries, something I cried and paid for at times.

I do feel that my two oldest children and my two younger children got two different versions of me as a mom. I enabled my first two children to think I owed them more because their father walked out of their lives and I never wanted them to feel that absence. I overcompensated and I paid for that in many ways that it became draining. Saying no is something I could never do because it made me feel that I wasn't a good mother. I had to learn while they were all adults that I had to set boundaries and that saying no was okay. I wish I did this when they were small children but being a parent doesn't come with a book.

My grandchildren have given me patience and a different kind of love. They are another reason why life is worth living!

I want to express that I love my mother even if we never had a good relationship. She was there for some things and for a lot, she wasn't. I believed she taught me to not take shit and to figure things out no matter what. I believe my mom did the best she could and she had her parents and siblings for support. I didn't have any of that. The only one who was there was my grandmother. She alone showed me that things were possible. She showed me unconditional love, never giving up, and no judgment. No matter how hard it is, it is possible.

I spoke with my children now that they are all adults. I asked them if they were OK with me writing this book. The fact that they said yes made it easy for me to tell my story.

Being a mom in a life of chaos trying to make it as normal as I could for them was the hardest thing to do. Trying to make them feel loved and safe and keeping a smile on their face was all that mattered to me.

My Letter to My Children
Just know that I loved you from the moment I laid eyes on each and every one of you. All of you were unique and had different bursting personalities. I am so happy GOD chose me to be your mother. I am proud of you all through the Bad and Good, just know I prayed and protected you the best way I knew how.

25

Healing after Abuse

"If I asked you to name all the things that you loved...How long would it take you to name yourself?" (Author Unknown)

SO many of us would never mention ourselves. I believe it comes from home first. We are to teach our children to love themselves and encourage them to become whatever they want in life. So many of us lived our life in survival mode because that was the only thing we knew.

We always complain about how complicated life is. But then, who doesn't feel this way? We are always making sporadic decisions and then complaining about the consequences. Now I will say that some things do come along that we have no control over and we are constantly tested. That can be very draining many times but it's the lessons that we are here to learn.

Many people would just say leave him but to leave you have to make a plan on how! Not knowing what the outcome is going to be is the scariest part.

I decided to make calls and I found a lawyer. I met up with the lawyer without my husband knowing. I had to think about how and when to serve him with the divorce papers. I was feeling afraid and thinking of who could help me. I had to think about who I could tell. If I told my friends or family, I felt like they would be involved in a mess and I didn't know what he would do to them!

When I finally left I had to learn to live alone and to find myself again. The last seven years have been a roller coaster and I realized that I have been choosing the same type of men: toxic and damaged. I feel like I was abandoned all my life. I feel like now I have become a person that attracts people who are broken and need help. My guilt and my heart make me feel important when I say yes to everything and give them everything I have: time, money, advice, shit even the shirt off my back. And I end up with nothing but pain and heartache. So many people take my pain as anger. That's crazy to me. I get told I need to heal and that I need a therapist because I'm not saying or reacting how they expect me to. It is still hard for me to express myself to others! But with everything it takes time.

Now I know what I deserve but I'm afraid to be vulnerable and I don't trust anyone. It's almost easier to partially love someone broken than whole because someone whole would make you take accountability. I've never had a healthy relationship. Not as a child or as an adult. Without experiencing that, how do we handle someone who is loving and has great intentions without questioning and overthinking everything? How do we break the cycle so that we can love and be loved properly?

You hear so much that we need to heal and we need to let go. It sounds easy until we are in a situation that brings about triggers. It's not that we want the new person to be responsible for helping us but they definitely need to be understanding. But what I find is that they say they didn't give you that pain. It's like a double sword because if they love you they can be there for you but you can't use them as the punching bag either.

Healing has helped me understand that staying angry doesn't hurt anyone but me. To hate all men doesn't make any sense and I was never bitter. I needed to love myself and make myself happy. It took me years to realize that I had to fix myself to move on.

I still believe in LOVE. Even though I thought love was fighting, yelling, and abuse to show that you cared. I know now that what I crave is healthy conversations, soft touches to feel safe, and reassurance.

I want women to know that they are loved and they don't have to stay. I know it's scary but know that you deserve happiness and peace and healthy LOVE. When you know what you DESERVE you will look at life differently and your perspective will be more clear.

My PURPOSE is to live my life to the fullest, to put GOD first, to be a good mother and grandmother, and to be kind to others.

Through everything that I endured, I want to express that life is definitely worth living. Focus on things that you want and move forward to make it happen. Because you have to understand that life goes on regardless.

All the time another woman dies because of domestic violence! This is starting to sound too familiar. When does this stop? Men need to do better and we should be protected. This awareness is for everyone who needs to understand that you need to value your life, you only get one! I believe that we need to support each other in the world, lift each other up, make people take accountability, and love more. There is so much hurt and so much hatred towards each other. We need to take the time to ask people if they are OK. We need to ask them, "How is your mental health?" We may not be able to fix people but we can definitely guide them to a healthier way of dealing with things.

The two men that I chose to love and have children with had something in common: They both resented who they were. Anger, sadness, blame. They never took accountability and I paid for their PAIN!

We all have a part to do small or big. It takes so much more energy to stay angry. Your thoughts are yours. You determine if your day will be a good one and how you react to negativity. Now is it easy? NO, but it's doable. See I have made so many mistakes. I never listened. I was stubborn. I thought my way was the only way.

I am grateful for the trials and tribulations as they created who I am today. **I have mastered survival and now it's time to live.**

My advice now to anyone who is going through this is to find someone you can trust and tell them everything, just in case something happens. Make sure to have a plan for your children in place! You can call the hotline for National Domestic Violence at 1-800-799-7233. Know that mental and physical abuse should never be tolerated. Find a way to walk away!

You really need to love yourself, put yourself in a safe place, and choose to be happy. If we do this, when life gets hard we can move forward and we are not looking for all of those things in other people!

26

Who Am I

You ask where I am now? I'm still putting it together. I've lost everything again and again and again. As for some of my family, I have learned they will not be there to help, not even during your worst times. But I'm grateful for the relationship I have with all of my four children. I'm 51 living and happy and finally at peace. I am grateful to have children that love me and now they are there for me while I find my way. Writing my story during my worst has been the best thing that's happened to me. I know so many people who die with lies and secrets because they are afraid to say the truth or afraid to ask to be told the truth. SET yourself free by being transparent with yourself. It's the best feeling. You owe that to yourself!!!

Who am I, you ask? Well, I am a strong woman with lots of dreams and dedication! I'm stubborn, I'm loving, I'm broken, I'm a fighter, a mother and grandmother. Most importantly, I Am Me.

I am an AUTHOR! I am a woman with a story that I HOPE helps you find another way to live your life with happiness, peace, and being strong enough to stand up for yourself. To do and get what you DESERVE! To open new doors but with the understanding that when some stay closed it's for good reasons. When things happen to you that you don't understand, remember to learn the lesson from it.

I am RESILIENT!

Resilient is who I have become after everything I've been through.

I love myself, but it took until right now to realize that. I will never let anyone ever make me question if I am enough.

I have met so many people who stop me just to talk and tell me their story or about their day and even a piece of their life and I have been able to listen with a smile. When some people might say, "I don't have time" or "shit, I don't know you," I say, "Why not?" I always feel blessed when people come up to me and share things with me. They may have a message for you. You may even save their life by just listening.

So many of us are told to let go of the past, but that is impossible. What we should be doing is not letting it affect us in the present, learning how to live, and building from it in a positive way. You have to realize this is how we become who we are.

About the Author

Daisy Plaza is a strong woman, mother of four children, and author. Daisy experienced trauma and violence in her home and community from an early age. Rather than letting this dampen her spirit, she used her experiences navigating trauma to help others on the front lines of the emergency room. In her writing, she shares her heartfelt stories of pain and healing to help others gain hope and strength.

Although her past may be haunting, she doesn't let that get in the way of building relationships with new people. Her extroverted nature is welcoming, yet intense, drawing many people to her naturally.

Daisy spends her days now continuing to heal and live her best life. She loves to hang out with all her wonderful grandchildren and is always connecting with her children. Daisy loves a nice place to sit and enjoy a chai latte, as she pursues her passion for writing.

Made in United States
North Haven, CT
12 June 2024